know the game

Men's H

Contents

Foreword

Hockey is a specialist pursuit. It can only be enjoyed if it is fully understood by players, umpires, coaches and spectators.

This valuable book makes a major contribution to that understanding. The information and advice contained herein should enable everyone to learn what is required of him, either as an individual or as part of a team.

I hope that the book will receive the attention and appreciation it deserves. By reading it, I trust that you will benefit and increase your enjoyment of the game.

Above all, I wish you well.

Phil Appleyard
President
The Hockey Association

The Game

Hockey, which appears to have had its origins in classical times, is a field game, played with sticks and a ball, between two teams of eleven players each. The object is to hit the ball between the goalposts of the opposing side. The side scoring the more goals wins the game.

Modern hockey may be said to date from 1876, when a few of the clubs, which played the game as it was then, formed a Hockey Union for the purposes of drafting suitable rules.

The Hockey Association came into existence in 1886 and in 1900 the International Rules Board was formed to make the Rules for the British Isles. In due time this Board became the International Hockey Rules Board which in 1980 combined with the Women's International Hockey Rules Board to form the Hockey Rules Board, which is an independent organisation within the International Hockey Federation, whose offices are in Brussels.

In 1975, the I.H.R.B. and the Women's International Hockey Rules Board joined forces to produce a single set of rules for both sexes. The current rules are the same for men and women and apply throughout the world.

Hockey is controlled by two umpires. Originally an umpire gave a decision only if appealed to by either side, but under the rules revised by the Board in 1900, they could in certain cases (for example, the 'sticks' rule) give decisions without appeal. As this led to frequent stoppages of play, in 1901 a note was added to the effect that the strict enforcement on all occasions of the 'sticks' rule might penalise the non-offending side, and umpires were asked to use their discretion. In 1907 umpires were given power to make all decisions without waiting for an appeal.

One of the earliest alterations in the rules was that prohibiting left-handed play. In 1904 intentional raising or undercutting the ball was prohibited, whilst in 1938 any form of interference with sticks, and the intentional use of the foot for the purpose of stopping the ball, were forbidden.

The last hundred years have seen changes which have largely eliminated rough play, and evoked a game highly skilful and scientific. Nowadays it is amazing to see the speed with which expert players can turn defence into attack by fast team-work and skilful passing.

The Field of Play

Dimensions and Size

Hockey is played on a rectangular ground, which should be 100 yards long and 60 yards wide. The surface should be level, close cut and well rolled.

It is not always possible to have a ground of the size required by the rules of the game, but it must be recognised that hockey is adversely influenced by fields of smaller area. It is more important to have the maximum width than the maximum length.

The Field of Play

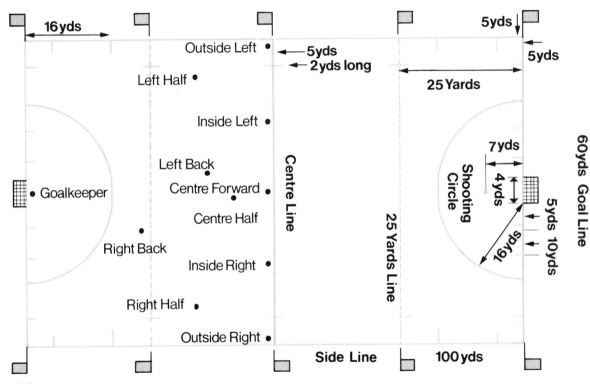

Fig. 1 Field of Play

Nowadays more and more 'all-weather' pitches with hard surfaces are being used and an increasing number of synthetic grass pitches are being constructed.

Playing Area and Markings

The playing area is enclosed by the side lines and the *goal-lines*. All lines shall be three inches wide.

When the ball passes wholly over the side-line a push-in or hit-in is taken by a member of the team opposed to the player who last played or touched it.

The *centre-line* divides the field into two equal parts. The game is started by a pass-back on the centre of this line, when all players must stand in their side's half of the field. A player cannot be offside in his own half.

There are two umpires.

The *goal-lines* are the shorter boundary lines at each end of the field of play. When the ball passes wholly over a goal-line, the game is restarted, unless a goal be scored:

(a) by a free hit by a defender from a spot anywhere up to 16 yards from the goal-line opposite the place where the ball crossed the goal-line if the ball was last hit by an attacker or sent unintentionally behind by a defender from a distance of 25 yards or more from the goal-line.

(b) by a corner, if a defending player unintentionally sends the ball over the goal-line from a distance of less than 25 yards from the goal-line.

(c) by a penalty corner, if a defending player sends the ball over the goal-line intentionally from anywhere on the field.

Twenty five yards lines are indicated by dotted lines drawn parallel to the goal-lines and 25 yards therefrom.

At a penalty stroke all players, except those taking part, stand outside the 25 yards area.

A white spot 7 yards from the centre of the goal mouth indicates the position from which a penalty stroke shall be taken.

The shooting circle in front of the goal consists of an area bounded by the goal-line and a white line drawn as follows:

A line four yards long parallel to the goal-line and 16 yards from the goal-line, continued each way by quarter circles having the goal posts as centres, to meet the goal-line. The inside front corner of the post is the centre of each quarter circle.

The shooting circle serves to indicate:

(a) The area within which the ball must be played by an attacker to score a goal.

(b) the part of the field within which the goal-keeper may kick the ball.

(c) the area outside which all players must stand (attackers outside the circle line, defenders behind the goal-line) when penalty corners are taken. The attacker hitting-in from the goal-line may however be within the circle at a penalty corner.

Flag Posts

These should be not less than 4 ft. nor more than 5 ft. high, and are placed at each corner and one yard beyond the extremes of the centre line.

The Goals

Each goal consisting of two perpendicular posts, 2 inches wide and 4 yards apart, joined together by a cross-bar, is placed at the centre of and touching the outer edge of each of the goal-lines. The minimum depth of the goal is 4 feet. Nets are attached to the goal-posts, cross-bar and ground behind the goal. Goal-boards not exceeding 18 inches high are placed at the foot of the goal-nets, the shorter boards being at right angles to the goal-line. They must not extend the width of the post either inside or outside the goal. Tubular goal-posts are forbidden.

Dress and Equipment

Hockey is a team game in which every man must be mentally alert and physically fit to pull his weight throughout the match, which is played at a fast pace for 70 minutes. Physical fitness, footwear and clothing are primary considerations.

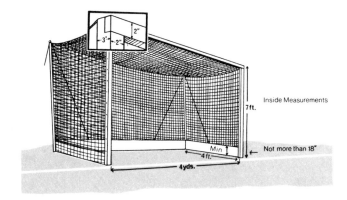

Fig. 2 The Goal

Dress

Most of the season the ordinary leather boots or shoes should be worn. They should be cleaned after every game, kept in good repair, and attention paid to the studs. Their function is to give a firm grip on the ground, which is necessary when changing direction. Rubber or nylon studded boots are preferable to the more traditional long studded boots as the latter do considerable damage to playing surfaces and ground maintenance equipment. Nylon multi-studded boots are the most suitable footwear for artificial grass surfaces, while training shoes are better on synthetic (e.g. rubber-type) surfaces.

Fig. 3 Note the equipment that is recommended to be worn in the modern game. Further details of dress and equipment are given at the end of the Rule Book (see 'Equipment Specifications').

The shirt, shorts and stockings should be in the club colours and kept clean. A spick and span team looks more business-like than one plastered with last week's mud and morale also tends to be higher. Equipment lasts longer if properly looked after.

A goalkeeper should wear pads and kickers which give adequate protection and fit the legs and feet comfortably. Pads must not be wider than 12 inches when on the goalkeeper's legs. He should also use an abdominal protector. Hand covering is a matter of personal taste. Special, but very expensive, goalkeeping gauntlets are made. These gauntlets must not be more than 8 inches wide when laid flat; there must be no webbing between the fingers; and any additional protection must be within the gauntlet itself.

Face-masks are now often used but an umpire will not allow one to be worn if he thinks it in any way dangerous. The plastic type is recommended by the F.I.H.

Sticks

Care is needed in selecting the stick. If weight and balance are unsuitable, progress in your game will be difficult.

Balance can be judged roughly by holding the stick with boths hands at the top of the handle and moving the blade up and down. See that the grain follows the curve of the blade as closely as possible. The grain is not always apparent in the Indian stick.

A stick weighing 18 to 21 ounces is adequate for the average person, but defenders may need a heavier one, which must not however exceed 28 ounces.

The stick should be cleaned after every game and occasionally wiped over with a slightly oiled or waxed rag. The stick, inclusive of surgical binding, if any, has to pass through a 5.1 cm ring.

The Ball

The ball used is one similar to a cricket ball, except that it is white. The ball may be seamless and other types of ball can be used by agreement between the two captains. It is not always possible to use the traditional leather ball so the International Hockey Rules Board have approved the use of balls made of other materials, such as plastic.

Rules of Play

Teams and Umpires

Hockey is played between two teams, each of eleven players. In addition up to two substitutes are permitted at any time during a game, though no substitute is allowed for a player who has so badly broken the rules as to be suspended, either temporarily or from all further participation in the match. (See Rule 1).

The team, especially in schools, often consists of five forwards (outside- and inside-right, centre-forward, inside- and outside-left), three half-backs (right-half, centre-half and left-half), two backs (right and left) and a goalkeeper. Numerically this is generally known as 1–2–3–5. As the inside forwards tend to work behind the others it is sometimes, and more accurately, known as 1–2–3–2–3. Since the late sixties more and more clubs and representative sides have adopted other formations – often called 'systems'. See page 38 for a fuller discussion.

There should be two umpires. Each takes his own half of the field and his own side-line. The Rules encourage them to co-operate with each other. Usually, therefore, an umpire will give decisions in the other half of the field when his colleague appears unsighted and near his own side-line. Even so, he should rarely need to cross the half-way line. Should he do so, he must be sure of being able to regain his correct position in his own half of the field should a rapid counter-attack occur.

An umpire may only award corners, penalty corners, penalty strokes and goals in his own half of the pitch. He may not award free hits in his colleague's circle.

Duration of the Game (See Rule 1)

A game is usually divided into two equal periods of 35 minutes each, though variations are permissible in certain circumstances.

Umpires should add at the end of each period time lost through stoppages for injury or other causes and all the time taken between the award of any penalty stroke and the resumption of play.

Start of Play

The starting bully has been replaced by a pass back. At the start of play, restart after half-time and after each goal is scored a pass back is played at the centre of the field. All players must be in their own half of the field and players of the opposing team must be five yards from the ball. The player taking the pass back may stand where he wishes.

The Bully

In the event of the game being stopped on account of an accident the game is restarted by an ordinary bully on a spot chosen by the umpire concerned.

In the circle a bully must not be taken within five yards of the goal-line.

Rule 10 (extracts)
(b) To bully, a player of each team shall stand squarely facing the side-lines, each with his own goal-line on his right.

Each player shall tap with his stick, first the ground between the ball and his own goal-line, and then, with the flat face of his stick, his opponent's stick, over the ball, three times alternately, after which one of these two players shall play the ball with his stick to put it into general play.
(c) Until the ball is in general play, all other players shall be nearer to their own goal-line than is the ball and shall not stand within five yards of the ball.

Fig. 4 The Bully

The essential points to notice are – first, that the players must stand squarely and use the flat face of the stick only to contact the other player's stick and subsequently to play the ball; and secondly, that all forms of tricky manoeuvre should be avoided, such as hitting the opponent's stick too hard, intentionally failing to make contact on the third tap and so on. Needless delay is often caused by attempted sharp practice.

The Push- or Hit-in (See Rule 17I)

For 'hit-in' read 'push- or hit-in' throughout.

When the whole ball passes completely over the side-line, it, or another ball, shall be placed on the line at the spot at which it crosses the side-line. The ball shall be pushed or hit-in without undue delay, by a player of the team opposed to the player who last touched it in play.

All players must be five yards away from the hit-in. Umpires are advised to show no undue lenience in this respect.

Penalty for Infringements

By the hitter-in – the hit-in is taken by the opposing team.

By any other player – the hit-in is taken again, except in the case of persistent offences, when a free hit may be awarded.

A free hit is also awarded against the pusher-in if he plays the ball again, or approaches within playing distance, before it has been touched or played by another player.

The Push- or Hit-in – Tactics

As with the free hit this is a moment of undisputed possession which must not be squandered. Yet many players do waste it either by lifting the ball or nor making the hit correctly. Both faults are inexcusable. Far too many teams fail to work at this tactic. Moves must be practised, the one actually to be used in a given situation being determined by the hitter-in. A simple method of signalling may be arranged. The hit-in should generally be taken by the wing half, though not if waiting for him to come up entails loss of time and opportunity, except over the twenty yards nearer to the opponents' goal-line. Here the wing forward takes it.

The players in close support of the half, the back, inner and wing, should retire the full five yards. In this, should opponents encroach, they are entitled to assistance from the umpire in enforcing the distance. The centre-forward and especially centre-half, who veer towards the hit, must be on the qui vive.

Basic coaching points are:

1. Take the hit-in as quickly as possible without losing possession.
2. Send the ball as far as possible from the hit-in point.
3. Team mates must move to offer or increase passing opportunities. Decoy running is often required.
4. Hitter-in to be assessing situation as he comes to take the hit. He must scan the whole area so as not to miss an unmarked colleague.

Illustrated (see page 12) are two of the many moves which teams can, and should, devise for themselves. None will work, except by luck, unless teams do practise them and unless players do move.

Corners (see Rules 15 and 17 II)

When the ball is sent out of play unintentionally behind the goal-line by a defender from less than twenty-five yards from the goal-line, a corner is awarded, unless a goal be scored. At a corner hit:

(a) the hit is taken by an attacker (usually the wing forward) from a spot on the goal-line within five yards of the corner flag.
(b) no player of either side may stand within five yards of the taker of the hit.
(c) Players of both teams may stand in the circle.

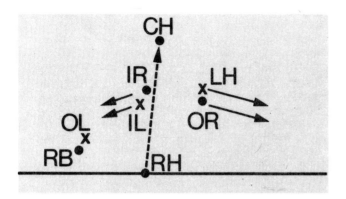

Long Corner Tactics

The corner should be treated as any other free hit. Space must be created by movement off the ball and support given to the taker of the corner. Variations can be applied.

In defence, players must be marked and the areas of greatest danger covered.

Scoring a Goal

To score a goal the ball must:
(a) be hit by or glance off the stick of an attacker, whilst in the circle, and
(b) pass wholly over the goal-line between the goal posts.

It is immaterial if, subsequent to being hit by an attacker, the ball goes into the goal off the person or stick of a defender. For further details see Rule 11.

If a defender fouls *and so prevents a goal* when taking part in a penalty stroke, a goal is awarded to the opposing team. (See Rule 16.)

The Push- or Hit-In

Fig. 5a (top): Outside- and inside-right moving to create space for hit to centre-half. If their markers do not move with them, the two forwards are open for a pass.

Fig. 5b (bottom): The centre-forward runs into the space opened by the decoy movements of the wing and inside.

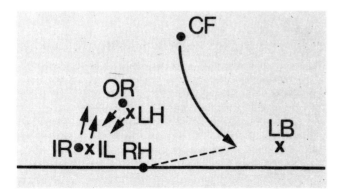

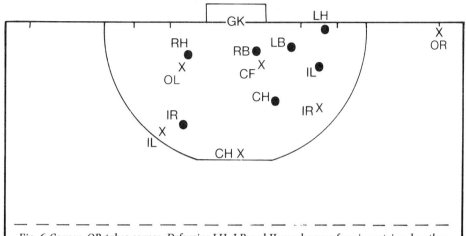

Fig. 6 Corner. OR takes corner. Defensive LH, LB and IL mark zones forming a triangle, other defenders man to man mark.

Free Hits (see Rule 14)

A free hit is awarded to the opposing team mainly for a breach of any part of Rule 12, excepting a breach by a defender in the circle. Then a penalty corner or penalty stroke is awarded.

Breaches of Rule 12 by a player include:

(a) Playing the ball with the back of the stick.

(b) Taking part in or interfering with the game without having his own stick in his hand.

(c) Playing a ball which is above his shoulder with any part of the stick.

(d) Playing the ball in a dangerous way, or in a way likely to lead to danger.

(e) Stopping the ball with any part of the body including the hand (excepting the goalkeepers in their own circles).

(f) Supporting the stick with the leg to resist an opponent.

(g) Kicking or carrying the ball.

(h) Hitting at, interfering with or holding an opponent's stick.
(i) Obstructing or interposing the body or stick as an obstruction to an opponent.
(j) Tackling an opponent from his left side, unless the player touch the ball before touching the stick or the person of an opponent.
(k) Charging, striking or holding an opponent.
(l) A goalkeeper kicking the ball whilst the ball is outside the circle.
(m) Dangerous or rough play, misconduct or time-wasting.

Umpires also have power to caution or suspend players if necessary.

Free Hits – Tactics

Certain principles apply in taking free hits.
(a) **Speed.** The whistle does not have to be blown before the hit can be taken, though opponents are allowed reasonable time in which to move five yards away. It is important to take the hit quickly before opponents can mark and cover. Speed does not apply only to the taker of the hit. His team-mates must also deploy swiftly so that he has the opportunity to pass usefully.
(b) **Penetration.** The hit which penetrates the opposing defence is best, but should only be used if the chances of maintaining possession are high. The more specu-lative hit may be used however, when, if successful, considerable territorial gain or a shot at goal will result.
(c) **Surprise.** Variety must be introduced. Sometimes the very speed of taking the hit will confer surprise; the man taking the hit may be able to mask his intentions – as by shaping to hit in one direction but actually hitting in another; and the movement of other players may open new angles.
(d) **Security.** This is vital in the Defence Area (i.e., the third of the pitch nearest the team's own goal), though sometimes a long hit into touch is valuable in relieving pressure. Security usually means retaining possession. Near the circle the hit across the centre of the pitch should be avoided.
(e) **Co-operation.** Often the man taking the hit is blamed for a bad hit when nobody had moved to offer him the possibility of making a good one. The taker of the hit must always be given close support. Teams frequently overlook the value of a supporting player being level with, or even behind, the striker.

At sixteen yards hits which are not too close to the side line the ball can usually be played square, providing that the wing forward on that side has come right back level with the hitter.

When defending against a free hit much of the foregoing applies, subject to the difference that possession has been lost. Thus defenders must apply the speed principle to block the hit. To do this they should aim to form an arc, probably at something like 10 yards range. They must also move rapidly to mark all the attackers, especially near goal.

If, in a given situation, it is frankly impossible to defend comprehensively, then security is observed by guarding against the most dangerous threat.

Fig. 7 Penalty Corner

Penalty Corners (see Rule 15)

For breaches by a defender inside the circle the penalty is either a penalty corner or a penalty stroke. A penalty corner is also awarded for a deliberate offence by a defender inside his twenty-five yards area but outside the circle. The principal points are:

(a) The free hit may be taken from any spot on the goal-line on either side of the goal, but not within 10 yards of a goal post.

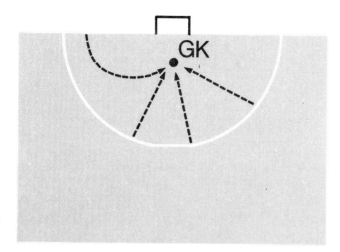

Fig. 8 Attackers moving to form an arc round goalkeeper to pounce on rebounds off him.

(b) Persistent breaches by the defenders will be penalised by the award of a penalty stroke.

Penalty Corners – Tactics

In Attack
Nowadays many games are decided by penalty ('short') corners. Surprisingly, most sides make no more than a token effort at practising them.

The Requirements

(a) A player who can push or hit out with speed and great accuracy.
(b) A player able to stop and either hit strongly and accurately, or move the ball to a better placed colleague.
(c) A follow-up wave keen to snatch at even a half-chance of converting a rebound should the original shot be saved.

The team of (a) and (b) MUST practise diligently together. Unless (a) is accurate, the whole operation is immediately jeopardised. The shot should be taken somewhere from opposite the centre of goal to a little way outside the line of the post nearer the pusher-/hitter-in. This ensures an adequately wide angle for the shot. It is now common to see experts striking from a yard or more inside the circle. Stepping into the shot gives greater power. Nevertheless, accuracy is the prime essential. The shot which goes straight over the goal-line is useless. Conversely, even the poorly hit shot which is on target forces a defender to do something and may easily present a conversion chance from a rebound.

Ideally every team should have two people trained to act as (a) and (b), so that a replacement can take over if one of the original two is unavailable or off form.

It must be stressed that *somewhere* between the hit-in and the shot the ball must be stopped – but not necessarily *immediately* before the shot.

The follow-up wave consists of all available players on

the circle and includes the hitter-in who must get on-side as fast as possible. The aim of this wave is to form an arc round the goalkeeper at two or three yards range.

Variations

A great many can be arranged, given sufficient practice. A huge repertoire is neither desirable nor necessary. Work at the standard drill. This is the one most likely to bring maximum profit.

Useful variations include:

(a) From the head of the circle the ball is played away to the left for either the hitter-in or for the advancing left-half to shoot. (Variation 1 in diagram.)

(b) The ball is passed across the circle for someone on the right to shoot. (Variation 2 in diagram.)

(c) The hit-in is made from the opposite side, i.e., from the attackers' right. (Variations 3 and 4 in diagram. In 4 because of the narrow angle, the ball is often passed into the circle, rather than a direct shot made.)

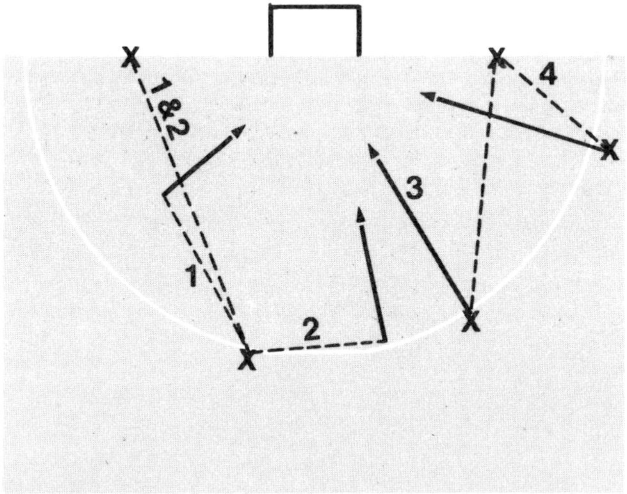

Fig. 9 For clarity the orthodox shot has been omitted

In Defence

The object of the Rule is to confer an advantage upon the attackers. They have the initiative. Given a sufficiently competent penalty corner team, they also have quite adequate time in which to make the orthodox shot at goal. Comparatively few shots score directly, but from the others there will often be a good chance of a follow-up goal.

It therefore follows that the defenders must aim to prevent their opponents scoring directly – by preventing the shot ever being made, if possible, or by saving it – or indirectly by clearing all rebounds. Though safety is paramount, the defendings should seize any chance to launch a counter-attack. This requires the help of their players coming back rapidly from over the half-way line.

Methods

There can be no infallible system. Even international teams use different ones. Ultimately the fate of the defenders rests on their hockey intelligence and skill. *The supreme requisite is that the goalkeeper and, whenever possible, the backs, have an uninterrupted sight of the shot.* Two possible methods are illustrated (see pages 18–19).

In A

(a) Player (1), someone chosen for his speed, takes the striker. He should try to tackle open stick and allow the goalkeeper a sight of the ball at all times. He must now allow himself to be beaten so that the attackers can advance on goal.

(b) Player (2), usually the right half, advanced 7–10 yards to the right of the post, offering cover to player (1). He will need to deal with any pass the striker makes to his side of the circle, and clear any rebounds off the goalkeeper's pads in his area.

(c) Players (3) and (4) are the post men, usually the full backs, but they must have a good eye for a ball and be confident and fearless. They advance 2–3 yards and must never let a direct shot pass into goal between them and their post.

   Both post men should be alert to cover any switches in the second phase of the corner as well as quickly readjusting to clear off the goalkeeper's pads should the need arise.

(d) The goalkeeper should advance as far as he can, usually 4–6 yards, allowing time to set himself for the

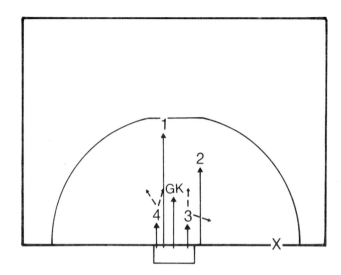

Fig. 10 Defence of penalty corner A.

shot at goal (that is, to get balanced). He may need to adjust his position should the attackers use a variation and shoot from an alternative position.

In A, the corner was 'injected' from the attacking left at X. If the penalty corner is injected from the other side, player (2) would start from outside the other post.

18

If the striker was standing very wide of the goal it may be that player (2) would take the striker and player (1) would offer the cover.

In B, the defending side are defending against attackers who they think are likely to switch the ball at the top of the circle and use a variation.

(a) Player (1) takes the striker or receiver, making sure that he does not allow himself to be easily beaten.
(b) Players (2) and (3) advance 10–12 yards and are prepared to cover the switches left or right into their areas of the circle. Both will offer cover to player (1), but player (2) on his open stick has a better chance of a covering tackle.
(c) Player (4) is the post man, covering the left post. As before, he must not allow a direct shot between him and his post.
(d) The goalkeeper covers the middle of the goal and the right post. He should advance 4–5 yards to narrow the angle.

It is essential that, whichever system is adopted, all players in the team know the role expected of each position so that an injured player's place can be taken by someone else.

The forwards must try and get back to help the defence in the circle if at all possible. If the defence can get possession and pass the ball to the forwards, excellent attacking opportunities should exist.

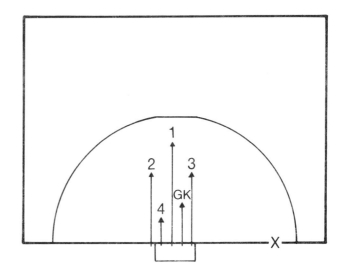

Fig. 11 Defence of penalty corner B.

At international and senior club level most goalkeepers prefer option B, because they come out 7 or 8 yards and if a shot is likely they lie down covering the centre of the goal and the right hand post. Special protection and a great deal of practice are essential and junior players should not attempt this.

19

Penalty Stroke (see Rule 16)

A penalty stroke is awarded:

(a) where a defending player commits a deliberate breach of Rule 12 or 14 inside the circle, such as:
   (i) the goalkeeper preventing the attackers from playing the ball by lying on it;
   (ii) obstruction in front of goal;
   (iii) interference with or holding the stick of an opponent who is about to shoot;
   (iv) 'sticks' by the goalkeeper or other defender to save a goal, or
(b) when a goal would *probably* have been scored if an unintentional breach of Rule 12 inside the circle had not occurred.
(c) for persistent breaking of the goal-line by defenders at penalty corners. (Rule 15(c).)

If any of these situations arise, the umpire must award the penalty stroke without hesitation.

The penalty stroke consists of a push, flick or scoop stroke taken from the 7 yards spot by a player on the attacking team who, when taking the stroke, shall stand close to the ball and who shall be permitted in making the stroke to take one stride forward. He may touch the ball once only and thereafter shall not approach either the ball or the goalkeeper. If the goalkeeper has been incapacitated or suspended a substitute may be nominated by the captain of the defending team, and may change his dress.

The goalkeeper must not move his feet until the stroke is taken. The attacker must not feint or take the stroke before the umpire blows his whistle.

Until the penalty stroke is completed all other members of both teams must remain beyond the nearer twenty-five yards line.

The game is re-started on completion of a penalty stroke
(a) by a pass back on the centre line when a goal has been scored or awarded or
(b) by a free hit at the centre of the pitch 16 yards from the goal line when a goal has not been scored or awarded.

All teams should have at least two proficient penalty stroke takers. They require much practice in achieving accuracy, in using body movements fairly to deceive the goalkeeper and in developing power. The flick is the preferred stroke and the best targets are the corners of the goal.

The goalkeeper should stand with his heels on the line, as this, whilst complying with the regulations, does offer some chance of saving a shot he has only partly stopped. If he holds his stick in both hands he is free to let go with whichever hand he needs to stop a high ball.

Should he stop a ball going into goal above shoulder height with his stick, a goal will be awarded. He should remember that he is allowed to catch the ball. (See Rule 16(d) (iii) and (e) (iii).)

Offside (see Rule 13)

As in other field games an offside rule is necessary. Players should note the following points carefully:

(a) A player can be in an offside position only if he is in his opponents' half when the ball was last played by a team-mate.

(b) If a player is offside, he is not automatically put onside by returning to his own half to play the ball.

(c) The material point is where the player was when the ball was hit or pushed in by a player of his own side and not where he is when he plays the ball.

(d) At the material time a player is in an offside position:
  (i) unless there are at least two opponents between him and their goal-line, or
  (ii) unless the ball when played by a team-mate is nearer to his opponents' goal-line than he is.

(e) A player in an offside position must only be penalised:
  (i) if he interferes in any way with an opponent or the play, or
  (ii) if, in the umpire's opinion, he gains some advantage by his position.

(f) The playing of the ball by an opponent puts the player onside, if, in the umpire's opinion, he is then not interfering with the opponent or the play.

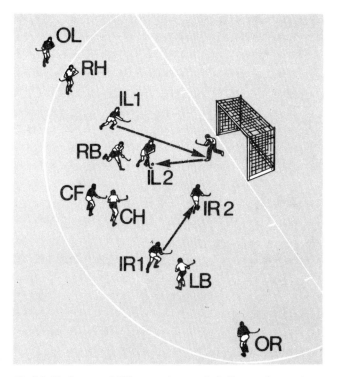

Fig 12: IL shoots and GK saves, clearing the ball towards IL, who shoots again. IR, having followed up after the first shot, is in an offside position when IL shoots again, and as he is interfering with the play of the GK, he is given offside.

The Strokes

The Hit

Grip the stick with both hands close together near the top of the handle with the two 'V's formed by the thumbs and forefingers pointing down the handle. The thumbs should be round the handle. A strong grip with the left hand is advisable. The left arm should be kept fairly straight throughout the stroke, elbows free of the body.

The ball should be a foot or so from the left foot and about in line with it. The head must be over the ball, the eye on it and the left shoulder pointing in the direction it is intended to hit, the head being kept down until after contact. When hitting a stationary ball, the weight will be evenly balanced on both feet. On the backward swing it will be transferred to the right foot and then to the left as the hit is completed. It is often helpful to step into the shot. When hitting a moving ball, the weight will be on the left foot with the knee bent.

The Hit

The speed at which the ball will travel is controlled by the tightening of the wrists at the moment of contact.

The hit should be made quickly and firmly. Take a short back swing and keep the left arm straight after the ball has been struck, checking the follow through if necessary by turning the right hand over. The right wrist and forearm should be firm at the moment of impact.

Do not attempt to hit the ball with one hand on the stick. The only occasions when one hand may be used are in the jab, lunge tackle or in collecting a ball at arm's length. The feet must always be in correct relationship to the ball. When not in possession of the ball, hold the stick with the left hand at the top of the handle and on the left side of the body, or across the body with the right hand lower down the handle, ready for instant action. To practise in pairs set up a cricket stump or post and from distances of five to twenty yards, aim to strike it. Practise both with a stationary and moving ball.

The Push

The Push

The push stroke and the flick are closely allied. In the push stroke the ball is moved by the drive of the stick along the ground, whilst in the flick it is made to rise. Keep the left hand at the top of the handle, the right hand half way down. More weight is on the left foot, the head being well down over the ball and the left knee bent. The ball is literally pushed along the ground. Try to keep the blade in contact with the ball as long as possible. The stroke is useful for short, accurate passes and in changing the direction of the game quickly and unexpectedly, making interception difficult.

The Flick

For the flick the right hand is low on the stick and the body crouched. It differs from the push in that the wrists are brought into play and the ball travels, not along the ground, but at about knee height, or above if necessary. The action of the wrists gives more power than in the push. The right hand moves as if it were turning a door knob, then opening the door; the left moves complementarily. For quick passing and close shots at goal, the right hand need not move so far down the stick. The flick is also used to lift the ball high over other players. For this the right knee must be very low.

The Scoop

This stroke lifts the ball over other players – usually opponents – out of their reach and thus free of interception. Its greatest tactical use is to drop the ball behind the rearmost defenders and is a method of combatting any attempted offside trap. In emergency it enables defenders to put the ball safely into touch.

It may sometimes be played from in front of the body as after a dribble. Its range is then limited. Generally it is played from the side of the body. If on the right, the hands change round on the stick. The left goes well down, gripping from above; the right holds the top of the handle. These positions are reversed for the left.

In both, the shoulders point roughly in the intended direction of the pass. The ball is about level with the toes of the front foot and a comfortable distance – say 12 to 18 inches – from them. It must be stationary when the stroke is played. This is done by sliding the bottom edge of the blade under the ball which is then hurled upwards and forwards with a shovelling movement. Do not snatch. Keep the blade in contact as long as possible. Power is derived from the synchronised movement of legs, hips, arms and shoulders. A skilled player, scooping from his right, will achieve distances of over 35 yards, though less from his left. Umpires will penalise any actually or potentially dangerous aerial stroke.

The Reverse Stick Pass

This should not be encouraged when a player has time to move his feet to play the ball with an open-side stroke. It can, however, be valuable in 'selling a dummy' and in concealing the short pass from left to right. The ball may be hit, pushed or flicked with the reversed stick.

With experience the pass may be made off either foot and with no alteration of the running action. The right hand is well down and the shots played with little back-lift or follow-through. In the push, power derives from the right hand and forearm, the stick staying in contact with the ball for as long as possible. In the flick, the ball is propelled off the ground by a flick of the wrists.

Gathering the Ball

In the air

Fielding the ball is an essential part of the game. If the ball has been struck so that it rises from the ground, it may be stopped with the stick, provided no part of the stick is above the shoulder, or with the hand.

Hold the stick with the left hand at the top of the handle, the right hand lower down. Collect the ball as far as possible in front of the body, the head over the ball at the moment of impact, ensuring the blade is in line with the ball. To minimise the rebound relax the right hand grip at the moment of impact, keeping the handle ahead of the blade so as to play the ball down.

On the Ground

If the ball is travelling on the ground, do not rely only on the lower part of the blade to stop it, since the ball may bounce and clear the blade. Use a 'straight bat' by holding the straight portion of the stick vertical and placing it in the line on which the ball is moving. In this way the upper part of the blade as well as the handle becomes available for stopping the ball should it bounce. The rebound can be minimised by moving the stick in the same direction as the ball at the moment of impact, or in the manner described in the previous paragraph.

Half-backs and backs receiving a pass or intercepting should gather the ball with the reverse stick only when there is an advantage to be gained by doing so or if they have no option. Forwards on the run, particularly inside-lefts, should use the reverse stick when collecting passes from the right in front of them so that their speed remains unchecked. Inside-lefts who collect and keep the ball on their right tend to "crab" thus losing forward speed. They also have difficulty in passing to the left without making it obvious and furthermore often tend to move in towards the centre-forward thereby crowding the middle and reducing the chances of scoring a goal.

The stick may be reversed clockwise or anti-clockwise. Practise both methods.

The Dribble

Dribbling is running with the ball under close control. Though important, especially to forwards, it can easily be overdone. Never dribble when a pass would be more effective.

The stick must be held close to the ball which should be

kept out in front of the body to avoid obstruction and to facilitate passes to either side. The body is bent in a running position but allowing the player readily to scan the field. Whilst the left hand remains at the top of the stick, the right goes down the handle for greater control.

The ball is moved in a succession of short taps, the open and reverse stick being used alternately. In turning the stick from the open face (used for moving the ball to the left) to the reverse, the left hand rotates it through the right and anti-clockwise. The right hand resumes its grip once the ball is on the reverse.

At first players should learn the movement of the stick and then, standing still, practise tapping the ball from side to side. This should be repeated at the walk, working up eventually to fast running. Zig-zagging may be introduced to improve control and competitions between groups, e.g., dribbling along a row of cricket stumps, about six feet apart, may be organised.

Beating an Opponent

An opponent will often best be beaten by passing, with or without first having to draw him. Sometimes, however, there will be no option but to beat him by taking the ball past him. This may be done on either his open (right) or reverse (left) side. Also, it is occasionally possible to feint so that he moves one foot from the other, the ball being propelled through the resulting space.

In essence all techniques depend on unbalancing the opponent by deception. Thus, if it is intended to pass him on his right, on the approach the weight is transferred firmly on to the right foot, inducing him to move his weight to his left to avoid being passed on that side. The right foot then pushes off for a powerful left side-step, the ball being taken through on the opponent's open side.

Conversely, to pass him on his reverse, the attacker feints left then moves the ball away, reverse-stick, on the defender's left. Salient points to remember are:

Control. Blade must be close to ball throughout. Sometimes, however, given sufficient space clear of interception by another defender, the ball may simply be pushed or hit past one side of the opponent and collected on the other.

The decisive movement should not be attempted at a pace too great for the attacker to exercise full control.

Timing. The critical moment comes when the defender is off-balance. It is fleeting; it must therefore be seized immediately.

The manoeuvres must start out of reach of the defender's stick, but if too far away from him he will have time to recover. The optimum distance is about four yards.

Avoid obstruction. At no time must the attacker interpose his body between ball and opponent.

The above basic methods deal with an opponent who is waiting to tackle. Refinements include luring an opponent into attempting a premature tackle. He is shown the ball. As he lunges at it, it is swiftly drawn away and then pushed past him in virtually one movement.

The Tackle

Tackling covers various methods of depriving an opponent of the ball. The three basic methods follow. In all, the following are important:

Determination. Mean to win the ball.

Timing. A premature tackle allows the opponent to move clear with the ball. The moment to tackle is when the opponent loses control of the ball, albeit only slightly. The great exception is in the circle; no opponent should be allowed to shoot.

Do not rush in. Exercise control and patience, possibly coupled with feinting, until your opportunity comes. Retreat if necessary, though not into the circle.

Weight. When waiting to tackle an on-coming opponent stand with your left foot slightly forward, evenly balanced and poised to move as required.

Eyes. Always on ball throughout. The attacker will try to use his body to deceive his opponent.

The Jab

The jab is made with the left foot forward – in emergency, the right – with the left hand behind the handle. Try to push the ball over the opponent's stick. The weight must not be so far forward that the tackler cannot recover to continue retreating should the tackle fail.

In feinting the same stroke is used to pretend to take the ball thus persuading the opponent into error.

Open Side Tackle

The stick must be firmly grounded. The right hand grips strongly, well down the stick, and traps the ball. These factors, aided by correctly placed body weight, make it extremely difficult for the opponent to retain possession.

Reverse-Side Tackle

Study Rule 12 II (c) which in high-class hockey is strictly enforced. The tackler must play the ball before touching stick or person of his opponent. Even after playing the ball if he does either of these things so as to obstruct his opponent, he will be penalised. The only sure way of complying with the Rule is to come in level with the ball. Certainly, any attempt at tackling from behind the opponent will invariably be disallowed. By the same token, the opponent must not obstruct the tackler. The stick is held in the left hand – no other way is possible – and the arm is extended across, but clear of, the opponent's body. The closed face of the blade traps the ball or lightly taps it away, so that the opponent runs past. A strong wrist and a particularly fine sense of timing are prerequisites for the most artistic of tackles.

After the Tackle

Making a successful tackle does not complete the player's task. He must then use the ball to the best available effect. In his own Defence Area and in the Build-up Area (middle third) this will usually mean a pass. Near the opponents' goal it may mean a dribble or a shot. Whatever the circumstances, the aim must be to bring the ball under full control in the least possible time.

Passing and Movement

Hockey tactics depend on passing and movement: passing to clear one's lines, build up an attack and to find and exploit gaps in the opponents' defence; movement to open angles for passes and to support team-mates in offensive and defensive roles. Surprisingly, considering the vast importance of both these skills, elementary faults go completely unremarked in many teams. Match analyses constantly show a great proportion of passes go astray.

Integration is the fundamental principle underlying all tactics. That is to say, when any member of a team has the ball the whole eleven are attacking; conversely when possession has been lost, all eleven are defending. Repeatedly squandering possession therefore limits attacking opportunities and hence the chance of victory.

In simple passing two people are involved, the giver and receiver. In more complicated passing others are also involved, as by running to draw away, or distract, defenders. When a marked man runs, his opponent must either go with him, thereby opening space, or let him go free to receive the pass.

Fig. 13 shows how, by running laterally and taking their markers with them, A and B open space for D to burst through, collecting C's pass.

Passer and receiver have equally important tasks. The passer must aim to give the receiver the ball how, when and where the receiver wants it and not pass merely to suit his own convenience. The receiver must ensure that the

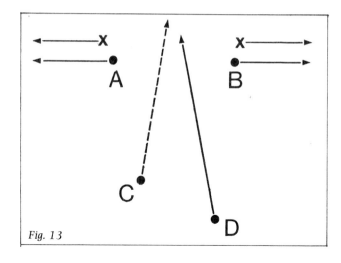

Fig. 13

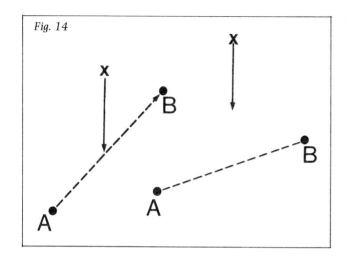

Fig. 14

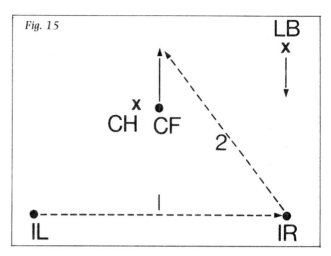

Fig. 15

pass he wants is in fact possible. Many players frequently ignore this point. They – and often enough the passer – do not allow for the movement of opponents.

On the left of fig. 14, B is too close to the defender who can move and intercept. On the right of the diagram, B has made the necessary effort to come back flatter to A so that X can no longer intercept.

B's fault is common. The most frequent reason is lack of thought, though another major reason is lack of sufficient fitness to undertake the considerable amount of running required in a fully integrated team.

All passes are either direct, i.e., to a man, or indirect into space for a team-mate to collect. A typical manoeuvre illustrating both sorts is shown in fig. 15.

Pass 1 is the direct, square from the inside-left to the inside-right. As the left-back advances, the inside-right then gives the indirect, pass 2, the through pass to the centre-forward.

In all passing one or more of the following principles should be observed:

(a) **Accuracy.** The more accurate the better. Even a minor inaccuracy may cause a precious loss of time while the ball is gathered during which opponents can close gaps in their ranks.

(b) **Space.** A sufficient space must exist so that no interception occurs.

(c) **Weighting.** Often a fine judgement and a good skill level are needed to ensure that the receiver of a through pass is able to bring the ball under control before he is tackled or before the ball goes into touch.

(d) **Execution.** The passer cannot execute the pass well unless he is controlling the ball. Moving at too fast a pace will prevent this. He must also choose the most appropriate method of propelling the ball and have confidence in his use of that particular stroke.

Having made his pass, the passer's duty is not finished. He must then move into the position most likely to bring maximum benefit to his team in the changed circumstances. Often this will mean moving to the close support of the receiver. Just occasionally it will pay for him deliberately to stand still for an immediate return pass.

Certain passing manoeuvres are known by specific names:

Dog-Leg Pass. This is used where the man with the ball wishes to pass to someone whom he cannot reach directly because of the positioning of opponents. He therefore uses an intermediate player. Typically, the centre-half may wish to find his right-wing, the immediate path to whom is blocked. The right-half receives the ball, swiftly transferring it, by virtue of the changed angle, to the wing.

A variation of this move occurs near to or just in the opponents' circle. A pass is hit quite hard at the intermediate player who simply glances the ball onwards for someone else to run on to and collect.

Triangulation. The name of this move derives from the path of the ball and the path of one of the two players involved. It is used by two men to beat one opponent, though quite often a second opponent may find himself eliminated.

The situation may arise with the wing-forward in possession but blocked by the opposing half. He therefore passes very flat – thus obviating any possible interception

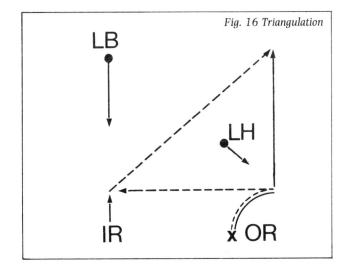

Fig. 16 Triangulation

LB

LH

IR

x OR

– to his inside. The inside then makes a through pass back to the wing.

Simple as the move seems, it frequently fails because the return pass to the wing is not placed out of reach of the half or is hit too hard for the wing to collect before it goes into touch. In fig. 16 the wing has made his approach to pull the half well out so that he cannot intercept the return. The diagram shows the optimum situation where the back coming up on the inside is beaten by the pass out to the wing so that both he and the half are eliminated.

In certain circumstances precise timing is required from the two forwards to avoid the wing being offside.

Wall Pass. Sometimes known as 'one-two', this is a simpler version of Triangulation. The player in possession in effect passes to himself like a ball rebounding off a wall, the 'wall' here being the second player.

Although it can be used on the lines of fig. 17, it can also be used successfully by a man coming from behind to get through the defence by using another, not too closely marked, forward.

Here the inside-left uses the centre-forward as the wall. If the centre-forward is too closely marked and cannot momentarily escape, he may be in danger of obstructing, a danger which would be increased if it were a player on his right using him as the wall.

In all passing the dual responsibility of both the giver and receiver cannot be over-emphasised; primarily, however, it is the clear duty of the giver to make matters as easy as possible for the receiver. For instance, it is stupid to crash a ball at a team-mate only a few yards away.

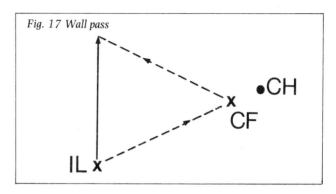

Fig. 17 Wall pass

Conversely, all passes should be made firmly. Far too many pushes and short reverse-stick passes are played so carelessly that they never reach their target.

Useful maxims for the giver of the pass are to look for the penetrating one first; if that is not on, make a safe one to retain possession; and, to stress the point, having passed, move.

Scoring (See Rule 11)

First and foremost all forwards, and any other player given the slightest chance, must want and be determined to score. Many goals are missed because players are not mentally prepared as well as from lack of skill. Players must be ready to shoot at the earliest opportunity, which is when the ball is fully on the line of the circle. By the same token, all attackers in the circle must eagerly seize upon any rebound. Defenders under pressure are much more likely to make a mistake.

Players practise shooting far too little. Footwork is essential. The aim should be to receive the ball with the feet positioned for the shot, or, when this is not possible, positioned so that the ball can be brought under control for the shot with minimal delay.

With time in which to shoot – and the greater a player's skill the longer his time – accuracy is more important than power. The high back swing gives time to the defence, who may just manage to push the ball away, and causes inaccuracy. In less favourable conditions the flick or push may be indicated. Any shot, even if mis-hit, is better than none at all. Faults are best avoided if at the critical moment the player concentrates wholly on his stroke and ball and makes a special point of keeping his head down.

The player at a very acute angle to goal should pass either across goal for a deflection or to a better placed team-mate. The worst thing he can do is to drive the ball into the sideboard. He will not squeeze the ball past a goalkeeper correctly positioned by the near post. Failing all else he may force the goalkeeper into conceding a corner or may offer himself the opportunity of following-up on to a rebound off the goalkeeper (fig. 18).

When a player receives the ball in the opponents' circle, like it or not, he also receives the responsibility of trying to score. Some players, unsure of themselves, make a pass subconsciously to rid themselves of this responsibility. If goals are to come players must not flinch from their duty to shoot. Whilst the value of correct foot-work has been stressed, in certain situations it is not always possible. Practising must therefore cover shooting off the wrong foot.

Fig. 18 Following-up

The Attack

Starting positions are shown diagrammatically on page 4, though the insides must be close enough to support the centre-forward should he win the bully. As play develops, the forwards tend to move in 'W' formation, albeit a very flexible, and hence frequently lop-sided, 'W'. In general the insides form the base of the letter, but all players must be alive to any opportunity to strengthen the attack by changing position.

Maintaining width keeps the opposing defence spread, thus offering more chance of penetration. This chance is improved by quickly changing the direction of the attack, as by swift, accurate cross-passing. Such passes cause the defence to switch with a momentary loss of depth. This is the moment for a telling through pass. (See fig. 15, page 29.) Cross-passing from right to left – e.g., right-back/right-half to inside-/outside-left – requires more care than vice versa because the ball will be travelling across the forehand of defenders. Forwards can rarely expect to succeed on their own. Half-backs must help, but not at the expense of completely unbalancing their own defence. The right flank is intrinsically more suited to attack. This means that the left-half has a greater defensive bias than the right. Indeed the right-half can occasionally act as a sixth forward with considerable effect. Half-backs can also often be used by forwards for back-passes to get out of difficulty or to change the direction of the attack.

Surprise is an important factor. Variation of method

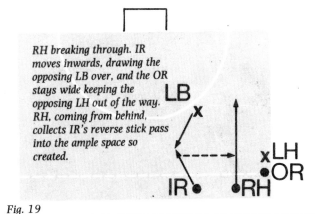

RH breaking through. IR moves inwards, drawing the opposing LB over, and the OR stays wide keeping the opposing LH out of the way. RH, coming from behind, collects IR's reverse stick pass into the ample space so created.

Fig. 19

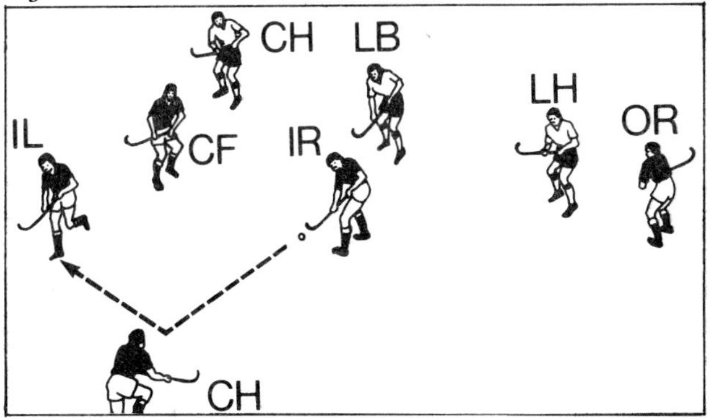

Fig. 20 *Inside-right in difficulties passes back to centre-half who passes immediately to inside-left who is unmarked.*

should therefore be introduced. For instance a wing-forward may centre early, from about the twenty-five yard line; or he may cut in, going straight for goal; or he may, having reached the goal-line, work along it into the circle.

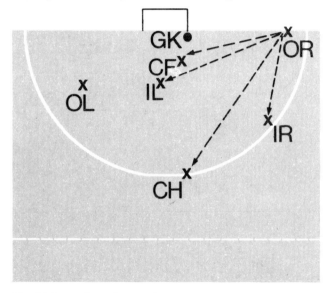

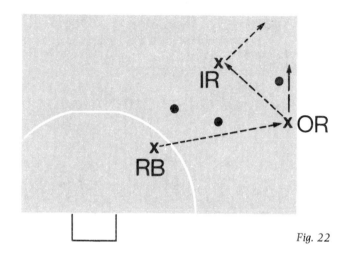

Fig. 22

Fig. 21 Passes from the wing forward in the circle near the goal-line. The outside-left picks up balls missed by, or deflected past, centre-forward and inside-left. The centre-half must come up in support and the forwards must exert some self-discipline to ensure passing angles are offered to the wing.

Should he achieve this position, which is of greater danger to the opponents, other players by movement and anticipation should ensure that they open as many passing angles for him as possible, as illustrated (fig. 21).

This particularly applies on the right. On the left, the wing will often find his inside, who should not be too distant from him, with a reverse-stick pass.

When a team has been under sustained pressure and possession is regained, they may find their opponents are over-stretched and vulnerable to a fast counter-attack. The urgent need is then to get the ball into the Build-up Area. Fig. 22 shows one possibility.

On any break it is most important that at least one man makes every effort to give close support to the player with the ball. It is immaterial who gives this support. In the diagram, for instance, it might well be the centre-forward. Should, in other circumstances, a defender come up into the attack, another player should take over his position to maintain the balance of the team. Thus, in the manoeuvre just mentioned, of the right-half passing through between his inside and wing, the wing may take his place by moving inwards behind him.

Tactics can be worked out – but will usually need much rehearsal and practice before they will succeed in match-play – for given situations. In essence, however, there should be a complete understanding throughout the team. Every player ought to know what to do when he is in possession of the ball, when a team-mate has it and when an opponent has it. Because of the need for fluidity in interchanging positions every player except the goal-keeper should be able to play competently in at least two neighbouring positions. A wing forward, for example, ought to be able to play reasonably well at wing half and inside.

All attackers must have the skill and confidence to take on a defender, be eager to score goals and have the necessary techniques to do so.

Some of the important points in forward play are:

1. Mental alertness to anticipate moves and rapidly to assess the situation.
2. Quickness off the mark, though sustained speed can also be needed.
3. Ability to use space to receive passes and to create space for others. A simple, but neglected, method of making space is to move with the ball in one direction, then to pass the reverse way into the now vacant space.
4. Readiness to go to meet the ball.

The Defence

As soon as possession of the ball is lost the whole team must realise that they have all become defenders. By being mentally alert they can anticipate this moment and save vital time in moving to deal with the new phase of the game. Especially in the Defence Area – that third of the pitch nearest their own goal – security is paramount. In defence, the over-riding aim is to stop opponents from scoring. A secondary aim is to launch a counter-attack once possession is regained, but no risks are permissible in the Defence Area.

In an intact standard defensive deployment, halves and backs mark individual forwards. The backs take the insides, the wing halves the wing forwards and the centre-half the centre-forward. The centre-half carries a special responsibility as the key-stone of the defence and, more than anyone else, has opportunity by shrewd passing to bring the forwards into action. It is particularly important that he of all players should not be drawn out of position because of the danger of uncovering the centre of the pitch. As a guide, he should not go within about ten yards of the side-line.

Halves and backs should mark their 'own' opponent and not be drawn from him. Distant from their own goal, halves do a lot of marking by intercepting passes. Near their goal they – and notably the centre-half – must not be lured into going for interceptions they cannot quite reach. This will eliminate them from the defensive system. The same consideration also applies to backs and no defender should rush into a tackle with little hope of winning the ball for the same reason. Opponents playing the ball in front of the defence are far less dangerous than when they have penetrated by getting a man in possession behind them. There is, however, one vital exception to this tackling rule. No opponent, whether the defender's 'own' man or not, must be allowed to shoot. The defence must always guard against the immediate threat.

The other task of backs and halves is to maintain depth in the defence. This entails covering and the avoidance of being caught square. Traditionally half-backs maintain depth among themselves by the wing halves pivoting on the centre-half. This, however, is a flexible concept. It could be, for instance, that both centre-half and one wing half were upfield supporting an attack. Depth would then be provided by the other wing half. Covering means that if a defender has been beaten, there is another defender behind him. Hence, an opposing wing who has beaten the half will find his way to the circle barred by the back. The danger of being caught square has already been illustrated under 'Passing and Movement' where the centre-half and left-back are simultaneously beaten by the pass of the inside-right.

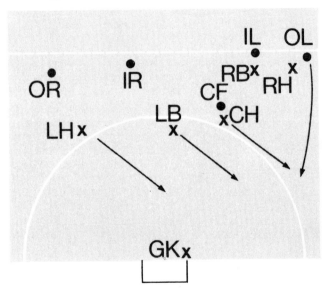

Fig. 23 The defence slides right to meet a very dangerous threat. The right-back, anticipating a pass to his inside from the wing, has moved up, but the wing has beaten the half and, with him, the back. The centre-half must deny the circle to the wing, the left-back and the left-half covering. The left-back hopes to engage the centre-forward should the wing attempt to pass him.

Experience will help players to form the fine judgement sometimes required in evaluating the demands of marking and covering. Admittedly this can be very difficult. (Indeed the problem led in soccer to the idea of a free back [sweeper] who undertook covering while the defence element in front of him did the marking.) Nevertheless, observance of the principle of guarding against the most dangerous threat will often decide the action to be taken. For instance the opponents may have broken through on their left past the defending right-half. The whole defensive formation must then slide right to contain the threat (fig. 23).

In particular the left-half will leave the right-wing, moving backwards and inwards to maintain depth by covering. He will also be able to engage the inside-right if necessary. This player is potentially more dangerous than his wing who, for the time being, is the least menacing of all the attackers. Before any pass could reach him, there would be a little time in which the defence could adjust their position.

A special word needs to be said about the backs in modern hockey. Traditionally, they were expected to move considerable distances up and down the pitch to mark the opposing insides and to cover each other. One isolated defender well in rear of his team-mates is now very vulnerable as forwards are allowed under the 1972 change to the offside rule to lie much further up-field. The present tendency is for the backs to remain in closer touch, not undertaking the long switches which were once a feature of their positional play.

Inside forwards have always been charged with tackling back and harrying the opposing insides in the Build-up Area. Often nowadays this defensive role is emphasised, compensating for the modification in the play of the backs. All forwards, however, have some task in defence. In the Attack and Build-up Areas wings and centre-forward will tackle back and harass opponents. Should the opposing attack progress beyond their reasonable reach, they will deploy so as to be available for passes out of defence. Wings must be willing to go deep into their own half of the pitch.

The Goalkeeper

A sound, rather than spectacular, goalkeeper can do much for a team's morale. He needs to be agile, possessed of quick reactions, dauntless and decisive. He must be able to kick, hit, flick, push and scoop well. For stopping low shots he should rely primarily on legs and feet, for higher ones hand and body. The stick is reserved for emergencies. He should try to kill any shot on his pads by letting his legs give a little on impact. The ball is then within reach for a stick clearance.

Very frequently, as with the ball running into the circle ahead of oncoming forwards, he will clear by kicking. Generally he should aim for the side-lines for greater safety. When he has sufficient time and can do so with complete security he should try to clear constructively to a team-mate. The most powerful kick is with the instep but the side of the foot can be used for kicking square to avoid interception.

Kicking, stopping and clearing can be practised with the aid of friends with a plentiful supply of balls. These are served to the goalkeeper by rolling, throwing, flicking, etc. Indoors a tennis ball can be kicked into the corner of a squash court to improve footwork and balance.

'Narrowing the angle' has been referred to under the defence of penalty corners. A goalkeeper on his line offers the maximum target for a shot. By advancing towards the shooter he reduces the target on each side of his body. The angle is thereby narrowed. This theory underlies the method of dealing with the forward breaking through into the circle. The goalkeeper should meet him firmly on the edge.

A common failing is needlessly falling to the ground. This is an emergency measure only, for once a goalkeeper is down he is out of the game and usually in critical circumstances.

Systems of Play

So far positional play and tactics have been based on the traditional line-up of 1 (goalkeeper); 2 (backs); 3 (halves); 5 (forwards). Because the insides are generally behind the other forwards the numerical description of 1–2–3–2–3 is more accurate.

For five or six years up to 1972, more and more clubs and international teams began using other formations (called 'systems'), especially those including a covering or 'free' back ('sweeper'). This sweeper was protected by the then offside rule.

The 1972 change to that rule reduced the critical number of defenders from three to two. When, some fifty years previously, soccer had made a comparable change – and a comparison is relevant because of the basic similarities of the game – widespread tactical changes had followed. Very briefly, at first a third, a centre-back, joined the two to guard against the menace of the centre-forward lying upfield. Wing halves moved infield to mark their opposing insides, leaving the original backs free to mark the wing forwards.

To counteract the centre-back, two centre-forwards were used. This in turn led to yet another back being added. Certain countries studied and developed the use of the sweeper to give added cover, as mentioned in 'The Defence'. Even with four backs, it means that only six players were available to fill the positions of the original 5 forwards and 3 halves. Whilst the forwards retained the same generic name, the players between them and the backs became known as midfields or, in hockey, sometimes as links. Depending on which of these elements teams wished to emphasise, they most frequently played either three of each or two midfields and four forwards. Soccer coined many names for the various new positions – not all of which have been given – but, to avoid confusion, traditional names tend to be retained in hockey and are used

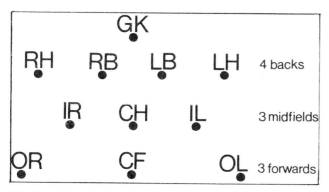

	GK			
RH	RB	LB	LH	4 backs
	IR	CH	IL	3 midfields
OR	CF		OL	3 forwards

Fig. 24

in this chapter. Diagrammatically, a hockey team playing what would be known as 1–4–3–3 could be represented as in fig. 24.

Where, however, a team uses four forwards, as in 1–4–2–4, it is common for the two in the middle to be referred to as left and right strikers.

Adopting a System

It must be clearly understood that departure from the orthodox does not per se command victory. No system can make up for lack of skill, lack of effort or lack of fitness, either physical or mental. In adopting a system the aim is to maximise the sum total of the team efficiency over that of the eleven individual players – as by developing strengths and hiding weaknesses. In a given match, such factors as pitch and climatic conditions and the known capability of opponents should be considered.

Tasks

There is a great deal of scope for the allocation of individual tasks, e.g. one man detailed off to close mark a particularly dangerous opponent. In general terms, however, for the 1–4–3–3, the outline tasks of the players would probably be:

Backs (RH, RB, LB, LH): Primarily defensive, working as a co-ordinated line giving depth rather in the manner of the traditional diagonal play of the halves. As circumstances demand, they will work in pairs, RH/RB, LB/LH, and especially RB/LB to maintain cover in the middle. Very likely RH will be given licence to break out to reinforce the midfields.

Midfields (IR, CH, IL): These again work as a team. They have the arduous duties of controlling the Build-up Area; initiating and supporting attacks; joining the forwards in the assault or to maintain attacking width; and, in defence, picking up opposing midfields and generally screening the backs.

Forwards (OR, CF, OL): Almost wholly attacking, though with harrying roles in the initial stages of an opposing attack. There must be far less adherence to the imaginary lanes up and down the pitch as taught to beginners. They will need to do much lateral running to support each other.

Support and Co-operation

At first sight it may seem that such a team is playing as three self-contained groups. This is emphatically not so. Every player has the responsibility of co-operating within the team strategy directly or indirectly with every other player.

Such co-operation is more readily understood when it is grasped that team tactics are based on triangles. Many triangles can be drawn between players all over the pitch. The most important, however, are those joining three adjacent players, e.g. RH, RB, IR and CH, IL, CF, etc. Each member of the triangle supports and co-operates with the other two.

The triangles are by no means constant. They change with the pattern of play. They change in number at once. The diagrammatic representation on page 38 shows the players in straight lines for simplicity, whereas they would be disposed in depth, providing more triangles.

The triangles will also change in shape. In attack the midfields are generally 'two-up', switching to 'one-up' in defence. (See fig. 25.)

These are only examples, for the relative positions of all players constantly vary. As players switch positions, as a well-drilled team can, constituents of the triangles vary.

A team working on these principles will find that defensive soundness improves; there is more attacking power and passing opportunities increase. In addition, where players have the skill to interchange positions the flexibility of the team is much enhanced.

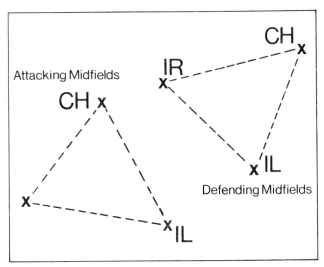

Fig. 25

Conclusion

Nearly all adult players should know the traditional formation reasonably well. The introduction of any new system calls for a great deal of effort and practice before it can be fully mastered and its potential developed.

Whatever the system, it is of fundamental importance that each man knows precisely his task in defence and in attack. Thus two teams said to be playing the same system can be found to differ widely in their interpretation of the roles of the individual players and therefore in their system.

Fitness for Hockey

Whatever the standard of player, be it the lower team in a club, a school 1st XI, a first class club side or a representative side, the higher the degree of fitness the more able the player will be to cope with the demands of the game. The onset of fatigue is the point at which skill standards drop, mental reactions become slower and the body is less likely to withstand any knocks. A high fitness level offsets these problems and makes the player more prepared to meet the demands of the game.

To delay the moment that fatigue sets in, the necessary supply of blood and oxygen has to be maintained to the muscles. Training to improve stamina, speed and strength will enable the body to cope with the problems of fatigue. In addition to these three, the hockey player requires the agility to react quickly, change direction and cope with the aspects of the game that require quick movement.

Physical fitness cannot be acquired a week before the game. It has to be built up over a period of time and then maintained, with extra training added if particular ceilings of fitness are required during a season for specific events such as knock-out matches, competitions, etc. The average hockey player rarely trains hard; more often he plays at training. To achieve the levels of fitness required for the modern game as much training as possible should be done with a stick and ball; but to acquire greater strength and speed it is necessary to get down to specific fitness work such as circuit training, interval work and weight training.

When training sessions are organised it is not enough just to play hockey and expect that this is going to result in greater fitness. To achieve higher levels of fitness the body has to be stretched to its capacity and the work load increased beyond that normally experienced. This requires practice that will achieve specific limits when properly carried out. These must be balanced so that various muscle groups are exercised in turn.

It is not proposed in this section to detail the sort of programme or the type of exercise that should be used as each player or group of players should seek the advice of an expert physical educationist. Training that has not been well prepared can be both dangerous and valueless.

What must be realised by all those playing hockey is that on the day of any particular game certain preparations prior to the starting whistle should be undertaken. The body is like a car engine and has to be warmed up before going into top gear. Often players need to move in top gear immediately after the game commences. The lack of thorough preparation can lead to damaged ligaments or torn muscles. The common scene of players standing round the circle hitting a solitary ball at the goalkeeper is totally inadequate. Players should ensure that their warm-up is thorough, that the various muscle groups of the body are stretched and that the heart is ready to undertake vigorous exercise. To do this properly takes 15–20 minutes of activity.

Facilities for training are becoming far more available with the increase in the number of sports halls around the country. The use of these facilities makes it possible to combine training with pleasure, e.g., a training session followed by indoor hockey. The development of competition in British hockey has made it necessary for more people seriously to consider their physical fitness and those clubs wishing to take this aspect of the game seriously, as all clubs ought, should make contact with their nearest H.A. Coach who will be able to advise them on methods of training suitable for the particular club and the facilities that they use.

Many training games involving small teams of three and four can be used to work on fitness and skill along with interval work including shuttle runs. *It cannot be stressed too often that to improve physical fitness means training hard. This is not always fun; but the end results are extremely satisfying and make the sweat and grind worthwhile.*

Hints on Coaching

The aim of coaching is to develop the potential of a player or team at the optimum rate. More and more English clubs are undertaking coaching and training sessions. Training is always better accepted when done in company, but the ambitious, dedicated player will have to do much on his own.

Techniques and Skills

Elementary techniques (sound and efficient actions e.g. hitting) become skills when other factors such as the presence of team-mates and opponents, the state of the pitch, etc., make the activity more complex. Coaching should be progressive, starting with the simple technique and moving through to the more complex, using the factors in 3, 4 and 5 below.

In coaching techniques and skills the coach will find that several may be taught and practised together, such as stopping/pushing. To cover the ground thoroughly he should observe certain principles. By far the most important is to talk as little as possible thus providing **maximum activity** for the class. He should proceed:

1. **Explanation and Demonstration.** A couple of sentences on the use of the technique, followed by a competent demonstration. He then breaks down the technique into component parts as affecting the player's body: head, feet, hands, body, weight transference. He may take the class through stage by stage.
2. **Practice and Criticism.** The class practise in convenient small groups, pairs, threes, etc. The coach must go round everybody, correcting errors in an encouraging manner. A general error may require calling the class together briefly.

3. **Opposition.** Should be introduced as soon as feasible, at first passive – e.g., a flag or stationary player – then, and more importantly, active. For instance, in dribbling the defender makes a genuine effort to win the ball.
4. **Competition.** Essential to maintain interest and to give students an aim. It can be quite simple – such as in stopping and hitting, which pair make the greatest number of clean stops in 2 minutes?
5. **Game-Like Situation.** There are many suitable small-sided games, several being suggested in 'The Grid', page 44.
6. **Any Questions?** To consolidate the instruction.

If a coach is running a day course he may deal with techniques in 15-minute spells. Especially where players are already of reasonable ability time may be devoted to practice games – 'conditioned' if necessary (see page 44) covering most of the techniques. The emphasis in the coaching of many sports is on more 'ball work'. This leads in tactical coaching to the necessity of maintaining possession, an impossibility without adequate skill.

Throughout, the coach should insist on a good standard of performance relative to the players' ability; any shoddiness should be rejected. He will find that he may need to vary his approach to individual students to bring out their best. He must ensure that the lesson is so organised that players do not have to stand about and, having set them working, that they keep up a high level of activity.

Skill is an early casualty of fatigue. Pressure Training – see also under 'The Grid' – takes this into account. It aims at developing concentration and the automatic, correct response from a player in a given situation. As it is also physically very strenuous, it trains players to maintain their skill level longer.

Coaching of Positional Play and Tactics

It is extremely difficult to coach all aspects of positional play, especially if the instructor is running a limited course, but it is hoped that the method shown below, although not exhaustive, will give the general idea.

Positional play may be divided into various groups:
1. Introductory stage – positional games.
2. Set pieces – bullies, corners, push-ins.
3. Basic tactics – the cross pass, the square pass, the through pass, the triangular pass and centres from the wings.
4. Individual positional play.

1. Introductory stage – For beginners. On a black-board or cloth model show the positions of the players on the field and the zones in which each player operates. Move to a field where stumps are placed on the goal-lines marking off the positional zones. Then have a game in which each player is prohibited from moving outside his own zone. If the game does nothing else it will show the instructor the need to concentrate on coaching the techniques.

2. & 3. Set Pieces and Basic Tactics

(a) Indoor work. The particular movement is worked out, using suitable aids, and questions answered, until the students have a good idea of this movement in theory.

(b) Outdoor work. The students move to the field and, where necessary, are divided into groups to practise the movement in which they have just been instructed. This should be done first at a walking pace and, when fully understood in practice, at the actual pace of the game. Opposition, at first passive but as soon as possible active, should also be introduced. *It is stressed that a few minutes practical work is far more valuable than many minutes of theory.*

The coach will require much patience in trying to build up a given tactic, however simple it may seem to him.

Coaching during a game. One method during a game, of coaching the movement learnt indoors and practised in the group, is by what is termed 'freezing'. The game, lightly umpired, should be controlled by the instructor who is armed with a powerful whistle. When that sounds, the players should 'freeze' where they are and the instructor can then point out the movement learnt, show its relationship to the game as a whole and criticise the individual players who have not executed that movement properly. Alternatively, a game may be stopped every ten minutes or so for comments by the coach.

Another method of coaching in a game in which one hopes to stress the importance of possession of the ball is by ignoring breaches of the rules with the exception of the one referring to obstruction (which must always be penalized or players learn bad habits) and for passing to a player of the opposite side. The mere threat of awarding a free hit for a blind pass will often be enough to improve greatly the standard of play. The instructor must stress that it is the duty of the player without the ball to be unmarked so that he can receive a pass.

Other practice methods are to have a 'conditioned' game where, e.g only the hit or the flick is allowed, or where the player receiving the ball is only allowed to give one tap after stopping it before he has to pass.

In all coaching the coach must use his imagination to devise schemes to cure the particular faults of the group being instructed.

4. Individual Positions

There is no infallible way of coaching the individual positions. The player must work much of it out for himself. The instructor can explain the fundamentals of a certain position during an instructional game (e.g., five minutes of a 'freezing' game may be devoted to, say, wing halves) but, if he is running a course where time is limited, then it is unwise to devote much of the course to coaching individual positional play. The coach may work alongside, or even temporarily take over from, the player concerned.

The Grid

A valuable training aid is the grid, a series of adjoining squares, 10 yards by 10 yards. It can be marked out quite

1 v 1. Goals scored by putting ball on opponents' line. Time 4 minutes.

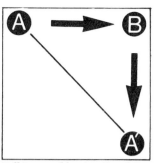

Ball is passed by A to B and B to A'. A moves across square to A', and repeats exercise back to A. Score one each time A returned to A.

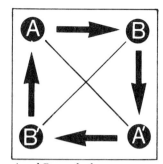

A and B now both move across the diagonals, the ball going round the square. One point each time the ball returns to A. The exercise is repeated with the ball travelling anti-clockwise.

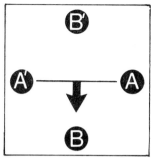

A moves across square and passes to B, A continues to A', B moving to B', passing to A at A', from the centre of the square. One point each time A returns to A. This is easily adapted so that the passes are made with the reverse-stick.

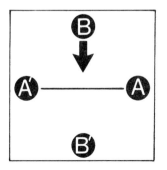

A starts running to A', B passes the ball so A receives in the centre of the square. A continues to A', then passes to B who is running to B'. The exercise continues. One point each time A returns to A. This is also easily adapted so that the pass is received on the reverse-stick.

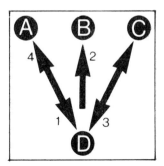

A, B and C serve passes to D. D passes to the player who is without the ball. Two balls are used, starting with A and C. Score: the number of passes D makes. Sometimes known as 'Target Man', this practice can be usefully used by the whole team for a few minutes to give them the feel of the ball and ground before the start of a match.

easily on any available space and lends itself to many training games and pressure training. The grid should be at least two squares deep.

The following are a few suggestions for improving ball control and, in most, accurate passing. Using a number of squares several 'teams' can compete against each other simultaneously.

The squares also provide convenient areas for small games to improve possession and movement off the ball. For instance a 3 v 1 game can be played. How many consecutive passes can the three make before the one touches the ball? When he does, he changes places with the person making the last pass. Play can be extended to two adjoining squares for, say, four or five agains two. 3 v 1 can also be played over two squares with the three having to stop the ball on one end line to score, whereas the one has only to push it over the opposite end line to score in a spell of 3 minutes. Hitting practice may require two or more squares.

In pressure training activities the player under pressure is placed in one of the boxes and any appropriate restrictions applied. He then performs the skill concerned rapidly a number of times. Thus, supposing the tackle was being taught, the rest of the team would in quick succession try to dribble across the box, the player there having to dispossess them somewhere within the ten yards. It is important for the coach to ensure that the tempo of the exercise is well maintained. He may need to take special steps to see that an adequate supply of balls is constantly available – as by detailing some players as fielders to retrieve and re-

turn to the attackers. Although the man in the box is the primary beneficiary, the others are also receiving profitable practice.

Lecturing

Though practical work far outweighs theory, lectures are needed, often to form the basis of outdoor activities. The following will aid the inexperienced coach.

1. **Preparation.** There is no substitute for comprehensive preparation. Stages at which aids are required should be carefully marked. Some coaches work from main headings; others from more extensive notes. Preparation also covers checking the facilities available.

2. **Construction.** Know what to say. Make sure the important points are covered and arranged logically. This is the main part of the lecture. It needs only a brief introduction but should be followed by a summary of the main points and adequate time for questions.

3. **Maintenance of Interest.**
   (a) **Delivery.** Avoid a monotonous voice. Speak brightly, deliberately rather than rapidly, use well-pointed pauses and make sure your voice carries to the back rows.
   (b) **Personal Habits.** Avoid any – such as pacing about – likely to distract.
   (c) **Humour.** Invaluable for 'refreshing' students, providing it is not malicious at the expense of one

of them. Much preferable is a joke at your own expense.

(d) **Visual Aids.** Of many sorts, apart from blackboard and chalk, such as films, slides, posters, cloth models. Use them to drive home specific items and not as an end in themselves.

(e) **Timing.** Avoid immediately after meals and avoid over-long lectures. 30 minutes talk is about all a class can usefully absorb.

4. **Questions.** Confine those from students to the end of the lecture, or at least to the end of the section. Insist that they are relevant to the topic. The coach's own questions aimed at consolidating what he has taught, should be directed to individual students by name.

Planning a Coaching Course

For maximum benefit courses must be carefully prepared so that all available time is properly used. The instructor should know beforehand the number of those attending and their playing positions and the indoor and outdoor facilities available. He should make certain that there is appropriate coaching equipment – such as a generous supply of balls, cricket stumps or flags, visual aids, etc.

Consultation with assistants is imperative before the course starts so that all know their part in the programme. This should as far as possible be capable of adaptation to bad weather and conditions. In certain instances the coach may be asked to concentrate on specific aspects of play, but often a good start to a programme is a short game. This allows a prelimnary assessment of the students. A general course might then go on to cover techniques. There is no need at all for those to be dull. Following the hints given in the previous section will ensure that interest is aroused and maintained.

According to the time available, the coach may follow with some or all of the set-picccs, c.g., free hits and penalty corners, and team-play. A suitable way to end will be a lightly umpired short game, primarily for the enjoyment of the players rather than for instructional purposes. The coach should do his best to involve representatives of the local Umpires' Association as both the Coaching Sub-Committee and the Umpires' Coaching Sub-Committee of the Hockey Association are anxious to work together at all levels. An instructor need not be a great player, but must have ample knowledge of the game at the standard concerned. He must be able to express himself simply, clearly and interestingly, be competent to detect and correct faults and not least be possessed of unlimited patience. Above all, any criticism must be constructive.

Should a coach require help or advice on any point he should apply to his County or Divisional Chief Coach without hesitation.

Further Information

World Hockey available from International Hockey Federation, Avenue des Arts. 1 (Bte 5), B1040 Bruxelles, Belgium.

Hockey Digest available from The Editor, Hockey Digest, 66 Lower Road, Harrow, Middlesex HA2 ODJ

The following are available from the Hockey Association Coaching Office, 6 St John's, Worcester WR2 5AH:

The Hockey Association Coaching Handbook, ninety pages on many aspects of the game (£3.50 including p&p).

The National Coaching Foundation Introductory Study Pack (£9.00 including p&p).

Rules Books: **Outdoor Hockey**
Indoor Hockey
Mini Hockey

A selection of the books available from the Hockey Association, 16 Upper Woburn Place, London WC1H 0QD, or bookshops:

The Science of Hockey. Horst Wein (Pelham Books)

Hockey – Teaching and Playing. Trevor Clarke (Lepus)

Hockey for Men and Women. T A Podesta (EP Sport, A & C Black)

See and Learn Hockey. Horst Wein (Swiss Hockey Association)

Better Hockey for Boys. Geoff Poole (Kaye and Ward)

The Advanced Science of Hockey. Horst Wein (Pelham Books)

The Young Hockey Player. Richard Charlesworth & David Hatt (Angus & Robertson)

Hockey. John Cadman and Chris Cox (A & C Black)

Hockey for Men and Women. Denis Glencross (Rigby)

Indoor Hockey. Sue Slocombe and Carl Ward (A & C Black)

Also recommended:

A Guide for the Hockey Umpire. Paddy Selman (Southern Counties Hockey Umpires Association). From W.J. Colwill, Birches, Chesham Lane, Chalfont St Peter, Bucks, SL9 0PG.

Notes for the Guidance of Umpires. Terry Podesta (Midland Counties Hockey Association). From Mr. J.W. Hadley, 43 The Friary, Lichfield, Staffs, WS13 6QH.

The Rose Award Scheme

This scheme has been set up to encourage personal performance amongst schoolboys and other young club players, leading in turn to further growth and development of the game. There are Senior and Junior Sections. In both, boys carry out a series of tests marked for accuracy and for speed. Based on their scores candidates are awarded badges, ranging from one rose up to five roses. These are national competitions.

Literature is available from the Co-ordinator, Rose Award Scheme, at the address of the Coaching Office.

All schools are encouraged to affiliate to the English Schools H.A.

Details are available from the Hon. Secretary: D. J. Newton, Kennedy's House, Aldenham School, Estree, Herts. WD6 3AJ.

Umpire Coaching

The senior officials of the H.A. Umpires Coaching Sub-Committee are:
Chairman: Wing Comd. J.K. Craven-Griffiths, O.B.E., SM26 (R.A.F.) Ministry of Defence, St. George's Road, Harrogate, North Yorkshire, HG2 9DB.

Hon. Secretary: R.L. Webb, 84 Main Street, Hardwick, Cambridge CB3 7QU.

The above will be happy to answer any queries on umpire coaching and to provide details of local officials.